CLAMS
IN THE SAND

KIRSTEN LAKE

PowerKiDS press.

New York

Published in 2018 by The Rosen Publishing Group, Inc.
29 East 21st Street, New York, NY 10010

First Edition

Editor: Melissa Raé Shofner
Book Design: Tanya Dellaccio

Photo Credits: Cover Joanna Cepuchowicz/EyeEm/Getty Images; pp. 3–24 (background image) Kemal Mardin/Shutterstock.com; p. 5 (top) Monontour/Shutterstock.com; p. 5 (bottom) littlesam/Shutterstock.com; p. 7 (top) https://commons.wikimedia.org/wiki/File:Stewart_Island_Oban_Mudflats.jpg; p. 7 (bottom) Paul Souders/Corbis Documentary/Getty Images; pp. 8, 21 (top) JIANG HONGYAN/Shutterstock.com; p. 9 Oksana Stock/Shutterstock.com; p. 11 (top) Daniel Gotshall/Visuals Unlimited/Getty Images; p. 11 (bottom) https://commons.wikimedia.org/wiki/File:Muscheln_mit_Sipho_Nahaufnahme.jpg; p. 13 Jodi Hilton/Getty Images News/Getty Images; p. 14 HikoPhotography/Shutterstock.com; p. 15 SNC Art and More/Shutterstock.com; p. 17 (top) Suzi Eszterhas/Minden Pictures/Getty Images; p. 17 (bottom) HASSAN AMMAR/AFP/Getty Images; p. 19 Jim Lavrakas/Perspectives/Getty Images; p. 20 Marilyn Angel Wynn/Nativestock/Getty Images; p. 21 (bottom) CWIS/Shutterstock.com; p. 22 SAHACHATZ/Shutterstock.com.

Cataloging-in-Publication Data

Names: Lake, Kirsten.
Title: Clams in the sand / Kirsten Lake.
Description: New York : PowerKids Press, 2018. | Series: Critters by the sea | Includes index.
Identifiers: ISBN 9781508162971 (pbk.) | ISBN 9781538325117 (library bound) | ISBN 9781538325827 (6 pack)
Subjects: LCSH: Clams-Juvenile literature.
Classification: LCC QL430.6 L35 2018 | DDC 594'.4-dc2

Manufactured in the United States of America

CPSIA Compliance Information: Batch #BW18PK: For Further Information contact Rosen Publishing, New York, New York at 1-800-237-9932

CONTENTS

LET'S LEARN ABOUT CLAMS!

Clams are mollusks, which are animals with soft bodies and no backbone. The word "mollusk" comes from *mollis*, which is Latin for "soft." Clams come in many colors, shapes, and sizes, but most are between 0.5 inch and 4 inches (1.3 and 10.2 cm) wide. There are more than 15,000 species, or types, of clams!

There's probably a lot you don't know about clams. For example, scientists think one species of clam called the ocean quahog is the longest-living animal on Earth. Some are more than 400 years old!

SEA CREATURE FEATURE

Giant clams are huge! They often grow up to 4 feet (1.2 m) wide. They can weigh more than 500 pounds (226.8 kg)!

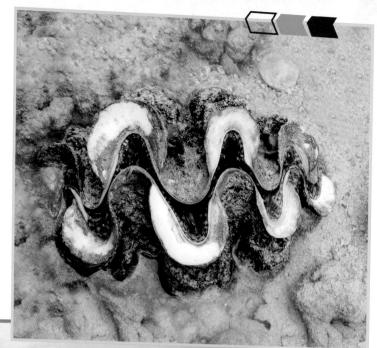

Clams are bivalve mollusks, which means they have two hard shells. Other bivalve mollusks include oysters, mussels, and scallops.

BURIED IN THE SAND

Clams can be found in different **environments** around the world. Some live on the sandy, muddy ocean floor. Others live on the bottoms of lakes, ponds, and rivers. These are called freshwater clams.

Giant clams live on **coral reefs** in the South Pacific Ocean and Indian Ocean. Pacific gaper clams live in mudflats along the Pacific coast of North America. Northern quahogs live along the Atlantic coast. Amethyst gem clams live there, too. They're very small and can be hard to see in the sand.

SEA CREATURE FEATURE

Mudflats are strips of land that are covered with seawater during high tide. The seawater leaves behind lots of food for clams and other animals.

Grizzly bears find clams in mudflats. Some eat clams whole, while others twist the shells apart with their paws. Others crush the clams with their teeth and spit out the broken shells.

PARTS OF A CLAM

Clams' shells **protect** their soft body. The shells are joined in the back. Two strong **muscles** help them open and close these shells. A thin, skin-like covering called the mantle covers a clam's soft body. The mantle produces the matter that makes up the clam's shells.

Inside their shells, clams have a heart, a stomach, and a muscle called a foot. The foot sticks out between a clam's shells. It helps the clam move around and dig in the sand.

SIPHONS

FOOT

SEA CREATURE FEATURE

Clams have two tubelike parts called siphons on their mantle. Food and water enter and leave a clam through its siphons.

Giant clams come in many different colors and patterns. Their shells have wavy edges. No two giant clams are the same!

EATING AND BREATHING UNDERWATER

Clams use **gills** to breathe underwater. While a clam breathes, it can also eat! Clams are filter feeders. Filter feeders are animals that keep water clean by eating **plankton**.

To eat and breathe at the same time, clams draw in water through one siphon. As the water flows in, the gills take oxygen from it. At the same time, tiny hairlike parts on the gills trap plankton for the clam to eat. The second siphon then pushes the water back into the ocean.

SEA CREATURE FEATURE

Clams can't live on dry land. They need to stay wet because their gills can only take in oxygen from the water.

Some clams bury themselves in the sand and keep only their siphons sticking out.

FROM BABY TO ADULT

Female clams use their siphons for more than just eating and breathing. They also use them to push thousands, sometimes millions, of eggs into the water. Clams produce eggs in late spring, when the water begins to warm. Only a small number of eggs will go on to become larvae, or baby clams. Of those, only a few will become adults.

Some young clams attach themselves to rocks or sand with byssus threads, which are special fibers they produce. Others dig into the seafloor using their foot.

SEA CREATURE FEATURE

The bump on the back of a clam's shell is called the umbo. This is the oldest part of a clam's shell.

UMBO

You can tell how old a clam is by counting the rings on its outer shell. The rings near the edge of the shell are the newest. Older clams have more rings.

DIFFERENT TYPES OF SHELLS

Some clams have very hard shells, while others have thin shells that break easily. Clams with thin shells often don't close fully because their siphons stick out the side.

Steamer clams have thin shells. They live in mudflats along the Atlantic coast. Pacific gaper clams, or horse clams, have hard shells. They have long siphons that let them live deep in the sand of Oregon's mudflats. Northern quahogs have hard shells, too. Another name for them is hard-shell clams.

SEA CREATURE FEATURE

Northern quahogs also have names based on their size. Small ones are called littlenecks. Larger ones are called cherrystones. Chowder clams are at least 3 inches (7.6 cm) wide.

Pacific razor clams have long, thin shells. These razor clams were found on a beach in Twin Harbors State Park in Washington.

PROTECTION FROM PREDATORS

Clams close their shells around their soft body to protect themselves from predators. Giant clams have special skin that can sense movement. They also have simple eyes that can sense shadows. If a giant clam senses danger nearby, it has time to close its large shell before a predator attacks.

Even with their protective shells, clams still have many predators. Starfish, crabs, and even snails eat clams. Hungry sea gulls sometimes drop clams onto rocks to break open their shells.

SEA CREATURE FEATURE

Walruses eat clams by sucking them from their shells. They can eat up to 6,000 clams during a single meal!

Otters float on their back and smash clams with rocks to get to the tasty meat inside.

GIANT CLAM

HUNGRY
FOR CLAMS

Many types of clams live along the Pacific coast of North America. In Washington, thousands of people go to beaches to dig up Pacific razor clams. To dig for clams, you need a shovel, a bucket, boots to keep your feet dry, and a state clam **license**.

Sometimes clams are overharvested. This happens when people collect too many clams, making it hard for the species to grow back. Some people raise their own clams. Clam farming is a big business in places such as Cedar Key, Florida.

SEA CREATURE FEATURE

Raising clams helps cut down on overharvesting. Clam farming is also good for the environment because clams clean the water as they feed.

Digging for clams, also called clamming, is a popular activity in Alaska. This boy is wearing special pants and gloves to keep him warm and dry while he collects razor clams.

SHELLS, SOUPS, AND SAUCES

People have used clams for many things throughout history. For thousands of years, Native Americans used clamshells to make beads called wampum. The beads served many important purposes. They could be strung together or made into belts.

People eat clams in many different ways. As far back as the 1700s, people made soups that are similar to the clam chowder we eat today. Clams can be fried, steamed, or eaten over pasta. A popular dish in Italy is **linguine** with clam sauce.

SEA CREATURE FEATURE

The beads of this Native American bag were made using clamshells.

Stimpson's surf clam, also called the Arctic surf clam, is a type of hard-shell clam. In Japan, the surf clam's foot is used to make a **sushi** dish called hokkigai.

SAVE THE CLAMS, SAVE THE WORLD

One of the biggest dangers to clams today is overharvesting. Changes in the environment cause problems, too. Even healthy clams can be affected by small environmental changes. Scientists study clams to learn important information about water **quality** where they live.

As one of the longest-living animals on Earth, clams give us an idea of what our oceans were like long ago. By studying clamshells, scientists can even make guesses about how changes in the environment will shape life in our oceans in the future.

GLOSSARY

chowder: A soup or stew usually made with seafood, often made with milk, bacon, potatoes, and other vegetables.

coral reef: The hard remains of coral animals that form a line in ocean waters.

environment: The conditions that surround a living thing and affect the way it lives.

gill: The body part that animals such as fish use to breathe in water.

license: An official paper giving someone the right to do something.

linguine: A type of pasta with pieces that are thin and flat.

muscle: A part of the body that produces motion.

plankton: A tiny plant or animal that floats in the ocean.

protect: To keep safe.

quality: A measure of how good or bad something is.

sushi: A Japanese dish made with rice and other ingredients, such as seafood and vegetables.

INDEX

WEBSITES

Due to the changing nature of Internet links, PowerKids Press has
developed an online list of websites related to the subject of this book.
This site is updated regularly. Please use this link to access the list:
www.powerkidslinks.com/seac/clam